Dear Student:

Congratulations! You have successfully attained the first level in achieving a standard of excellence in music-making. By now, you have discovered that careful study and regular practice have brought you the joy and satisfaction of making beautiful music.

You are now ready to move to the next level in your music-making. I want to welcome you to STANDARD OF EXCELLENCE Book 2. I also want to wish you continued success and enjoyment.

Best wishes,

Bruce Pearson

Practicing - the key to EXCELLENCE!

▶ Make practicing part of your daily schedule. If you plan practicing as you do any other activity, you will find plenty of time for it.
▶ Try to practice in the same place every day. Choose a place where you can concentrate on making music. Start with a regular and familiar warm-up routine, including long tones and simple technical exercises. Like an athlete, you need to warm-up your mind and muscles before you begin performing.
▶ Set goals for every practice session. Keep track of your practice time and progress on the front cover Practice Journal.
▶ Practice the hard spots in your lesson assignment and band music over and over, until you can play them perfectly.
▶ Spend time practicing both alone and with the STANDARD OF EXCELLENCE recorded accompaniments.
▶ At the end of each practice session, play something fun.

*The author wishes to thank fretted instrument specialist **Kevin Daley** for his contribution to this book.*

ISBN 0-8497-5973-0

KJOS NEIL A. KJOS MUSIC COMPANY, PUBLISHER

W22EBS

REVIEW

B♭ MAJOR KEY SIGNATURE

1 WARM-UP - Band Arrangement

▶ Use your left hand 1st finger when fretting 1st fret notes, 2nd finger for 2nd fret notes, 3rd finger for 3rd fret notes, and 4th finger for 4th fret notes. This is called playing in 1st position.

2 B♭ MAJOR SCALE SKILL

▶ Lines with a medal are Achievement Lines. The chart on page 47 can be used to record your progress.

3 BOTANY BAY

Australian Folk Song

▶ Remember to dampen the string on the quarter rest at the end of the piece.

4 DRIVE TIME

▶ When you see a page number followed by an arrow, *Excellerate* to the page indicated for additional studies.

5 SHEPHERD'S HEY

English Folk Song

REVIEW

E♭ MAJOR KEY SIGNATURE

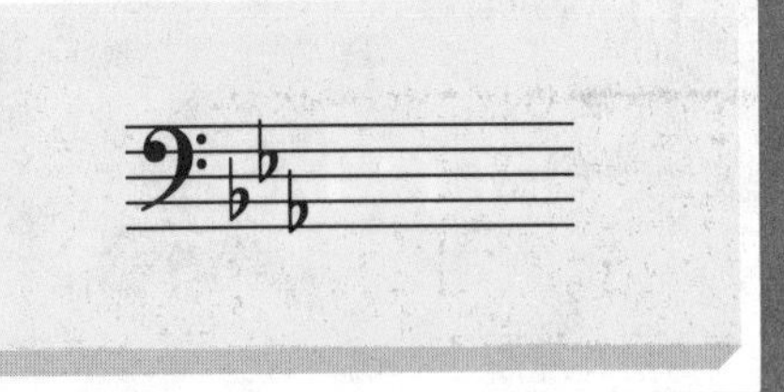

6 E♭ MAJOR SCALE SKILL

▶ To play D and E♭, shift your entire left hand so that your 3rd finger can play D on the 7th fret and your 4th finger can play E♭ on the 8th fret of the 1st string. *Shift your left hand so that your 1st finger plays C while ascending. As you descend, play C with your 1st finger, then shift back to 1st position so your 3rd finger can play B♭ and your 1st finger can play A♭.

7 MOLLY MALONE

Irish Folk Song

8 NO LOOKING BACK - Tacet

9 TURKISH MARCH

Wolfgang Amadeus Mozart (1756 - 1791)

▶ Remember to observe accents.

10 HYMN OF THANKSGIVING - Band Arrangement

Johann Crüger (1598 - 1662)
arr. Bruce Pearson (b. 1942)

REVIEW

F MAJOR KEY SIGNATURE

11 WARM-UP - Band Arrangement

Andante

▶ When notes appear on neighboring strings and are located on the same fret, press the lower note with the tip of your finger and the higher note with the pad of your finger. Roll your finger from note to note.

12 F MAJOR SCALE SKILL

Page 40

13 KNUCKLEBUSTER

14 GIVE ME THAT OLD TIME RELIGION

American Spiritual

15 ________________

Composer ________________
your name

▶ Compose an ending for this melody. Title and play your composition.

16 FOR ELECTRIC BASSES ONLY

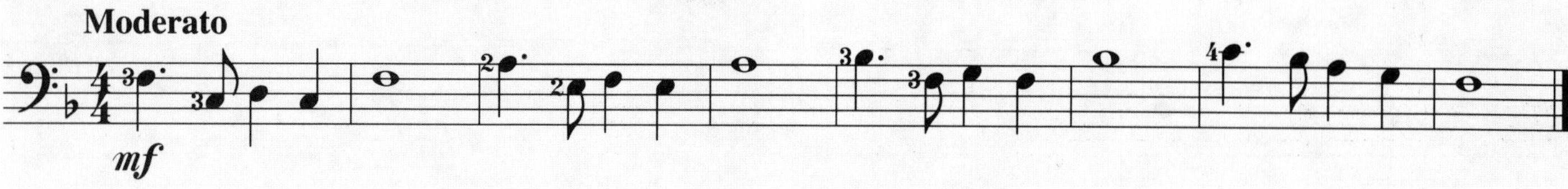

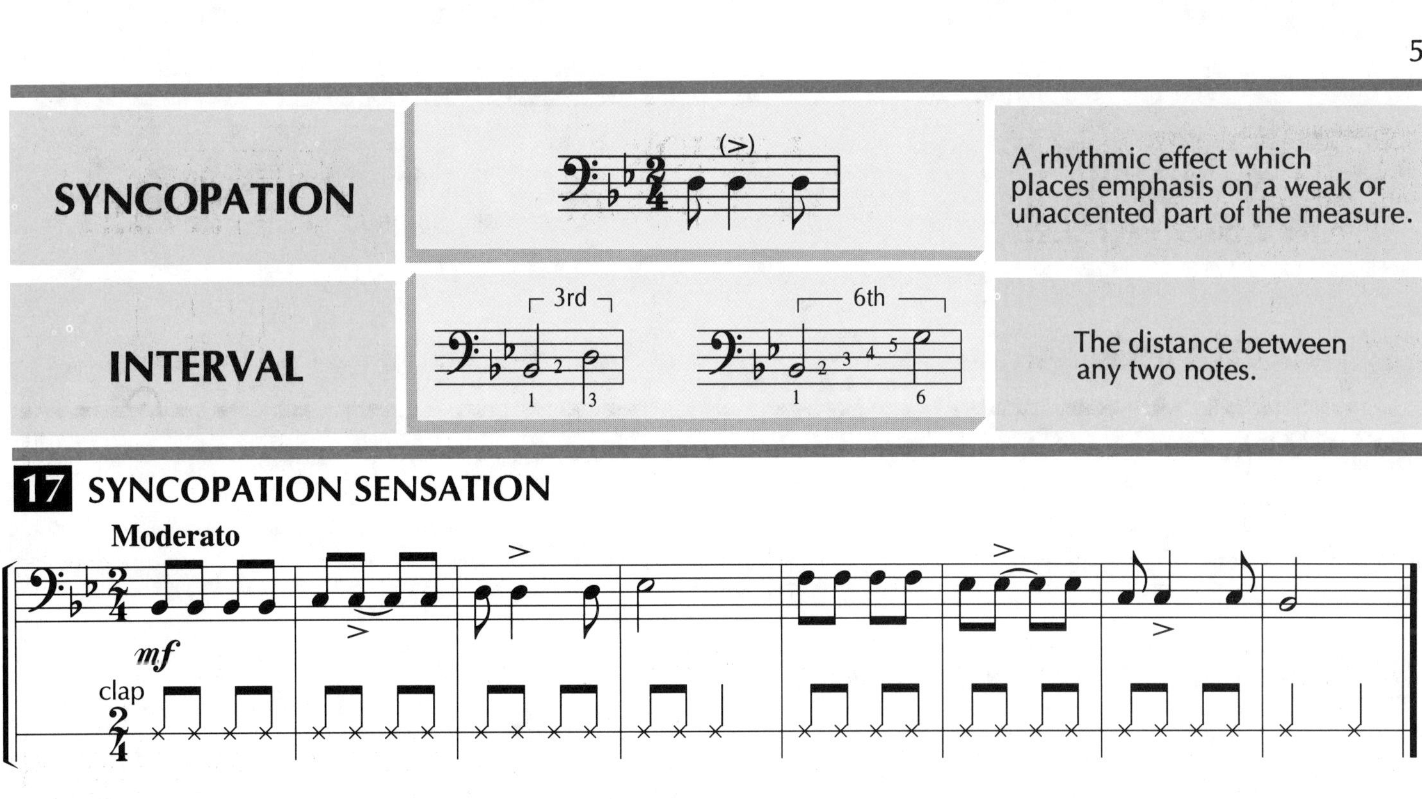

SYNCOPATION
(>)
A rhythmic effect which places emphasis on a weak or unaccented part of the measure.
INTERVAL
3rd
6th
1 2 3
1 2 3 4 5 6
The distance between any two notes.
17 SYNCOPATION SENSATION
Moderato
mf
clap

18 THE RIDDLE SONG
American Folk Song
Moderato
mp
4

▶ Write in the counting and clap the rhythm before you play.
19 NOBODY KNOWS THE TROUBLE I'VE SEEN
American Spiritual
Moderato
mf
20 INTERVAL INQUIRY
Page 40
2nd
3rd
4th
5th
6th
7th
8th or octave
1 2 1 2 3 1 2 3 4 1 2 3 4 5 1 2 3 4 5 6 1 2 3 4 5 6 7 1 2 3 4 5 6 7 8
▶ Sing this exercise using the numbers before you play.

21 GO FOR EXCELLENCE!
American Folk Song
Allegro
"Liza Jane"
mf
f

G MINOR KEY SIGNATURE

G minor has the same key signature as **B♭ major.**

TEMPO

Accelerando (accel.) **-** Gradually increase the tempo.

22 WARM-UP - Band Arrangement

Andante

23 G NATURAL MINOR SCALE SKILL

Moderato

24 G HARMONIC MINOR SCALE SKILL  **Page 40**

Moderato

25 MINKA, MINKA

Ukrainian Folk Song

Moderato

1. 2.

mf 2nd time - ***accel.***

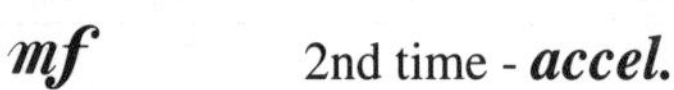

Hey!

26 LAREDO - Duet

Mexican Folk Song

Moderato

1. 2.

f

27 TURNING YOU LOOSE

Moderato

28 FOR ELECTRIC BASSES ONLY 

Andante

DAL SEGNO AL FINE (D.S. AL FINE)

Go back to the sign (𝄋) and play until the ***Fine.***

JOYEUX NOËL

Band Arrangement

French Carol
arr. Chuck Elledge (b. 1961)

Moderato

mp *mf* *mp* *p* *Fine* *mf* *f* *accel.* *mp* *mf* *rit.* *D.S. al Fine*

EIGHTH REST
= 1/2 count in 2/4, 3/4, and 4/4 time.
An eighth rest is as long as an eighth note.
30 EIGHTH REST ON THE BEAT
Page 40
Moderato
mf
▶ Write in the counting and clap the rhythm before you play.
31 EIGHTH REST OFF THE BEAT
Moderato
f
i m i m i m i m i m m i i m i m i m i m i m m i
▶ Remember to dampen on the eighth rests.
32 ACADEMIC FESTIVAL MARCH - Trio
Johannes Brahms (1833 - 1897)
Moderato
A.
f
B.
f
C.
f
33 BREEZIN'
Allegro
p
34 YANKEE DOODLE - Duet
American Folk Song
Moderato
A.
mf
B.
mf
35 FOR ELECTRIC BASSES ONLY
Moderato
mf
imimi i mi mimimmim

A♭ MAJOR KEY SIGNATURE

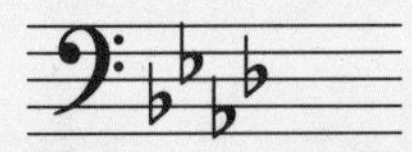

This key signature means play all B's as B flats, all E's as E flats, all A's as A flats, and all D's as D flats.

TEXTURES

Monophony - a single unaccompanied melody.

Polyphony - two or more melodies played at the same time.

36 A♭ MAJOR SCALE SKILL

37 GREASED LIGHTNING Page 40

38 PARTNER SONGS - Duet

▶ For an example of monophony, play line A or line B alone. For an example of polyphony, play line A while someone else plays line B.

39 GO FOR EXCELLENCE!

Stephen Foster (1826 - 1864)

ENHARMONICS

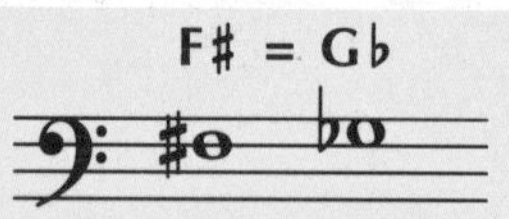

Notes that sound the same but are written differently.

ARTICULATION

Staccato (dot placed above or below note) - Play short and detached.

TEMPO

Allegretto - light and lively; slightly slower than **Allegro.**

40 WARM-UP - Band Arrangement

41 CHROMATIC CAPERS

42 SHENANDOAH

American Folk Song

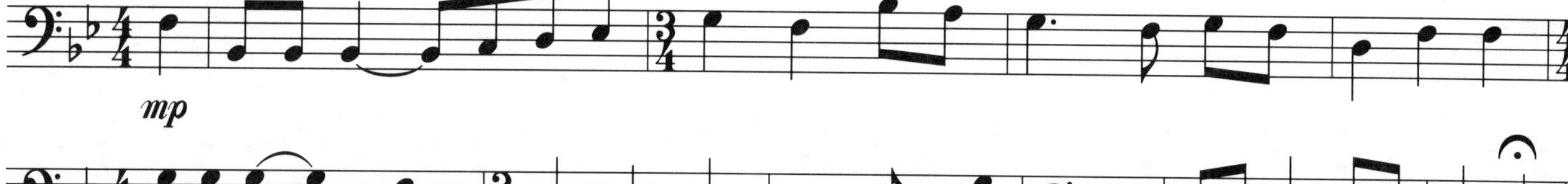

43 THEME FROM SYMPHONY NO. 94

Franz Joseph Haydn (1732 - 1809)

▶ To play staccato, pluck the string and dampen it immediately.

44 PARADE OF THE TIN SOLDIERS

Léon Jessel (1871 - 1942)

45 FOR ELECTRIC BASSES ONLY

Page 40

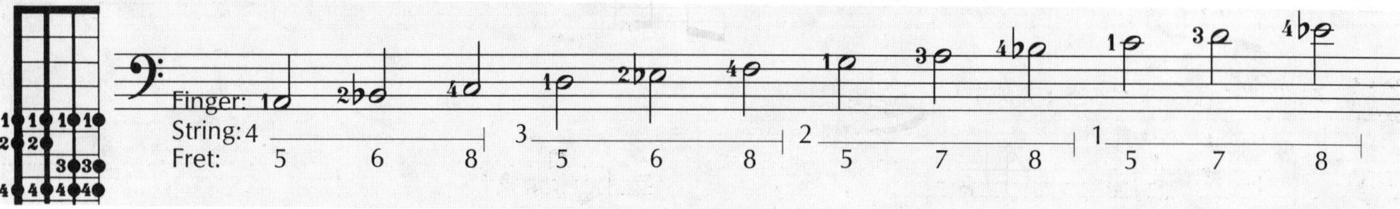

Many of the notes you already know in 1st position can be played in 5th position as well. In 5th pos., your 1st finger plays notes on the 5th fret, 2nd finger on 6th, 3rd finger on 7th, and 4th finger on the 8th fret. Play the notes in the diagram, paying close attention to the location of the notes, before playing in 5th pos. (If 5th pos. is not indicated at the beginning of an exercise, then play in 1st pos. as you proceed through the book.)

C MINOR
KEY SIGNATURE
C minor has the same key signature as E♭ major.
ARTICULATIONS
Tenuto (line placed above or below note) - Sustain for full value.
legato
Legato - Play as smoothly as possible.
46 C NATURAL MINOR SCALE
Andante
mf
47 C HARMONIC MINOR SCALE
B
Andante
i m i m i m i m
mf
48 MARCHE SLAV
Peter Ilyich Tchaikovsky (1840 - 1893)
Andante
1.
2.
mf legato
49 GREENSLEEVES Page 41
English Song
B
Moderato
mp legato
▶ Name the key in "Greensleeves." ____________________
50 JUBILATE
Wolfgang Amadeus Mozart (1756 - 1791)
Allegretto
mf
1.
2.
51 GO FOR EXCELLENCE!
Allegretto
mf

TEXTURE

Melody and Accompaniment - main melody is accompanied by chords or less important melodies called **countermelodies.**

52 WARM-UP

Andante

mf legato

53 HABAÑERA

Georges Bizet (1838 - 1875)

Andante

mf

54 SMOOTH AS SILK

Allegretto

5th pos.

f

55 HEY HO - Round (Canon)

Medieval Song

Allegro

5th pos. 1. 2. 3.

f

56 THE BRITISH GRENADIERS - Duet

English Folk Song

Allegro

5th pos. A. Melody

f

5th pos. B. Countermelody

f

▶ Remember to play A♭ with your 2nd finger on the 6th fret, 2nd string.

57 FOR ELECTRIC BASSES ONLY

Andante

5th pos.

mf

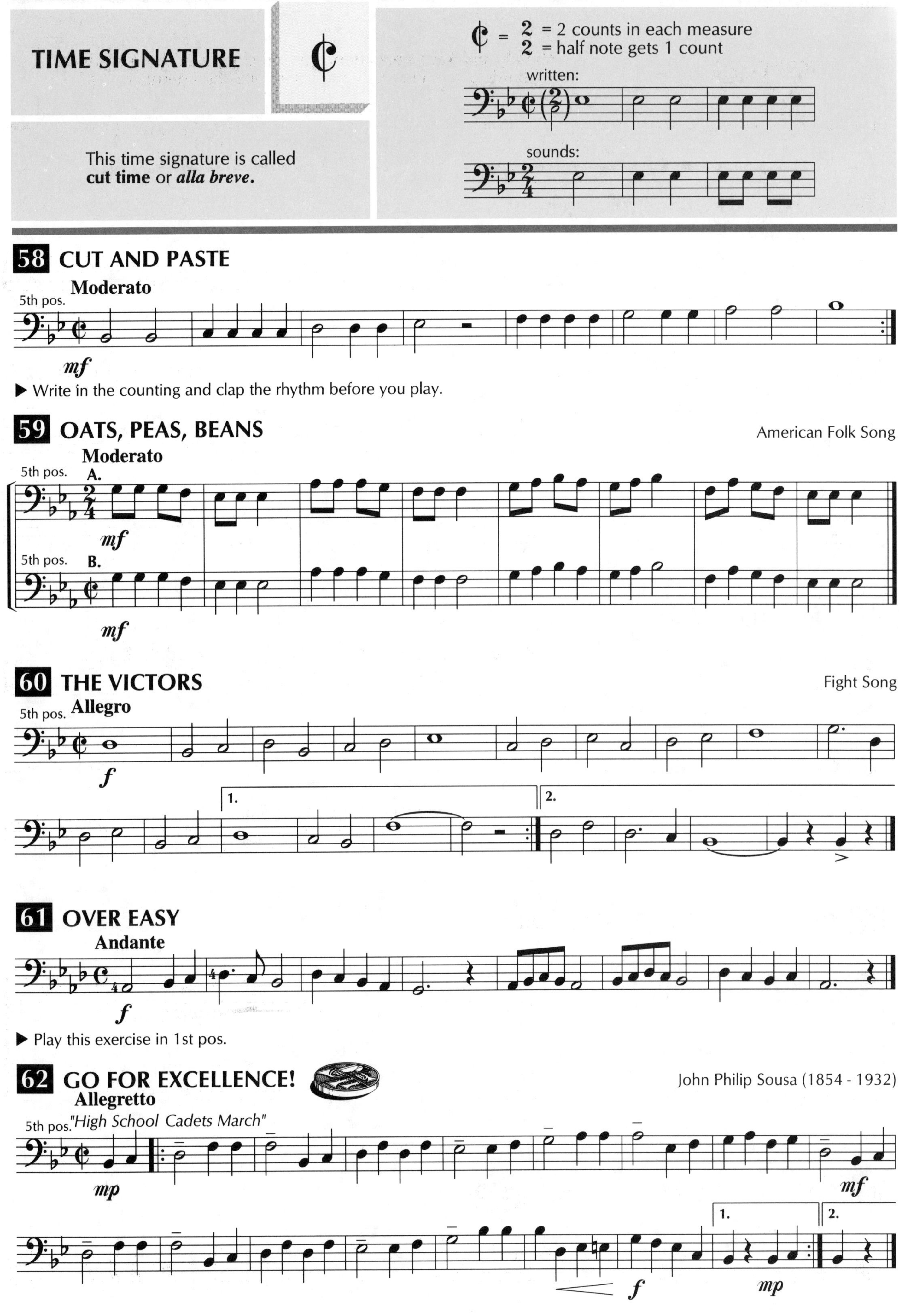
TIME SIGNATURE
¢ = 2 = 2 counts in each measure
2 = half note gets 1 count
written:
sounds:
This time signature is called
cut time or alla breve.
58 CUT AND PASTE
Moderato
5th pos.
mf
▶ Write in the counting and clap the rhythm before you play.
59 OATS, PEAS, BEANS
American Folk Song
Moderato
5th pos. A.
mf
5th pos. B.
mf
60 THE VICTORS
Fight Song
5th pos. Allegro
f
1.
2.
61 OVER EASY
Andante
f
▶ Play this exercise in 1st pos.
62 GO FOR EXCELLENCE!
John Philip Sousa (1854 - 1932)
Allegretto
5th pos. "High School Cadets March"
mp
mf
1.
2.
f
mp

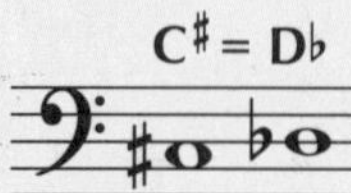

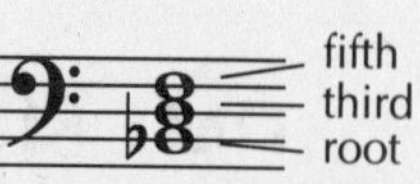

Two or more pitches sounded at the same time.

Andante

Danish Folk Song

Moderato

Reinhold Glière (1875 - 1956)

Allegretto

66 CHORD CAPERS

▶ Listen for the different types of chords played by the full band.

67 FOR ELECTRIC BASSES ONLY

Moderato

ENHARMONICS

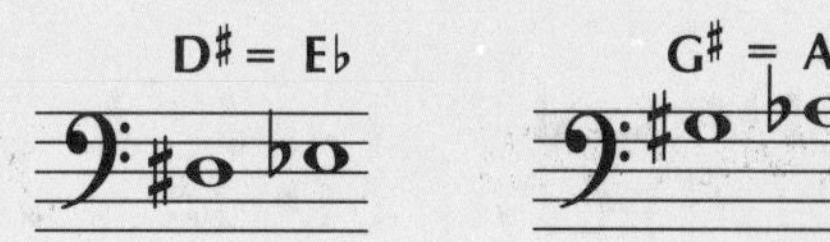

68 CHROMATIC SCALE SKILL

Page 41

69 SAILING THE HIGH SEAS

70 CHROMATIC MARCH

71 MANHATTAN BEACH MARCH

John Philip Sousa (1854 - 1932)

72 GO FOR EXCELLENCE!

DA CAPO AL CODA (D.C. AL CODA)

Go back to the beginning and play until the coda sign (𝄌). When you reach the coda sign, skip to the ***Coda*** (𝄌).

ROCK ISLAND EXPRESS

Band Arrangement

Chuck Elledge (b. 1961)

73 FINLANDIA - Band Arrangement

Jean Sibelius (1865 - 1957)
arr. Bruce Pearson (b. 1942)

74 TRIPLE PLAY

Permission granted for sale outside of the U.S.A. by Breitkopf & Härtel.

▶ Write in the counting and clap the rhythm before you play.

75 WE THREE KINGS

John H. Hopkins, Jr. (1820 - 1891)

▶ Name the key in "We Three Kings." ____________

76 GO FOR EXCELLENCE!

Page 41

This key signature contains no sharps or flats.

TIME SIGNATURE 6/8

6 = 6 counts in each measure
8 = eighth note gets 1 count

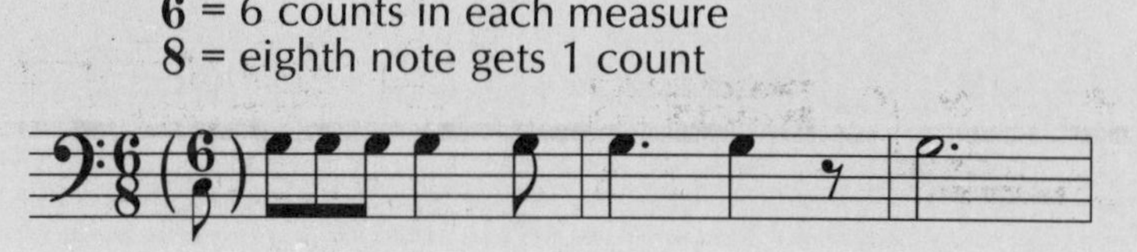

▶ Draw in a breath mark (’)at the end of each phrase.

▶ Practice slowly at first to keep an even tempo, especially when shifting to and from 5th pos.

80 UPS AND DOWNS

▶ Write in the counting and draw in the bar lines before you play.

81 FOR ELECTRIC BASSES ONLY

SIXTEENTH NOTES

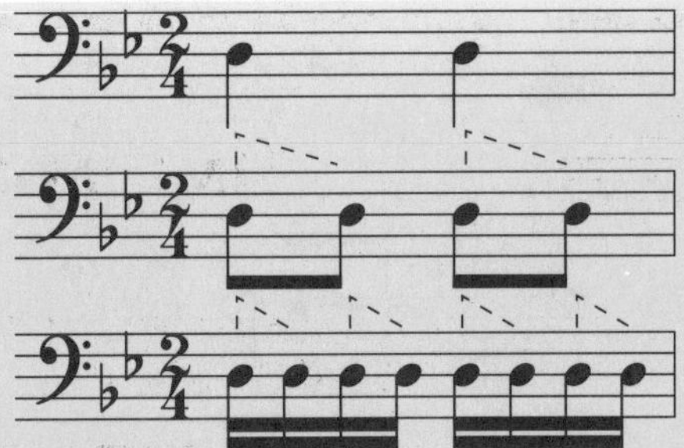

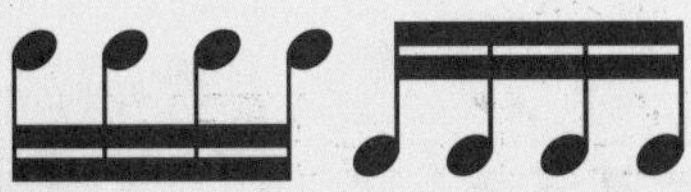

Two sixteenth notes are as long as one eighth note.
Four sixteenth notes are as long as one quarter note.

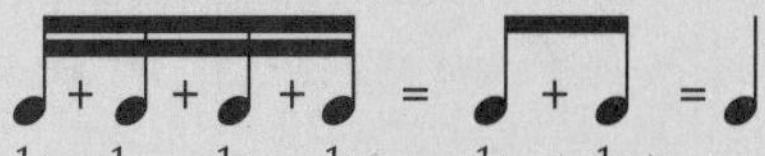

$\frac{1}{4} + \frac{1}{4} + \frac{1}{4} + \frac{1}{4} = \frac{1}{2} + \frac{1}{2} = 1$ count

Each sixteenth note gets $\frac{1}{4}$ count in $\frac{2}{4}$, $\frac{3}{4}$, and $\frac{4}{4}$ time.

82 WARM-UP - Band Arrangement

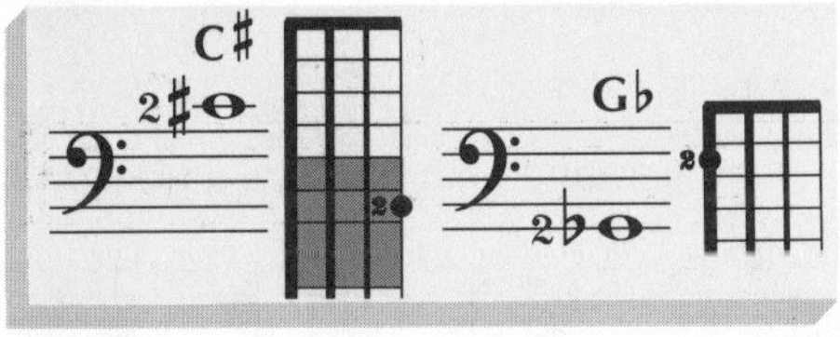

C♯ G♭

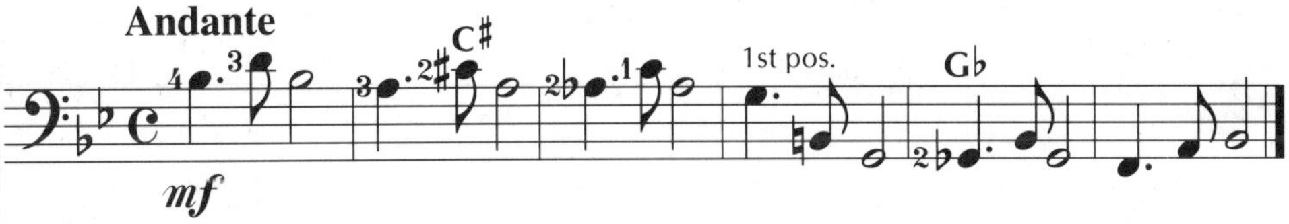

Andante

mf

1st pos.

83 COUNT ME IN Page 41

Moderato

mf

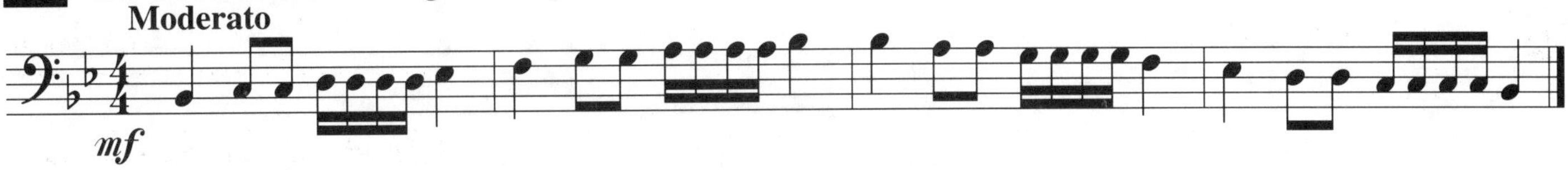

▶ Write in the counting and clap the rhythm before you play.

84 KEMO KIMO

American Folk Song

Allegretto

▶ Remember to alternate your right hand index and middle fingers.

85 FRENCH MARCHING SONG

French Folk Song

Allegro

▶ Name the interval between the first and second notes. ____________

86 FENG YANG SONG

Chinese Folk Song

Moderato

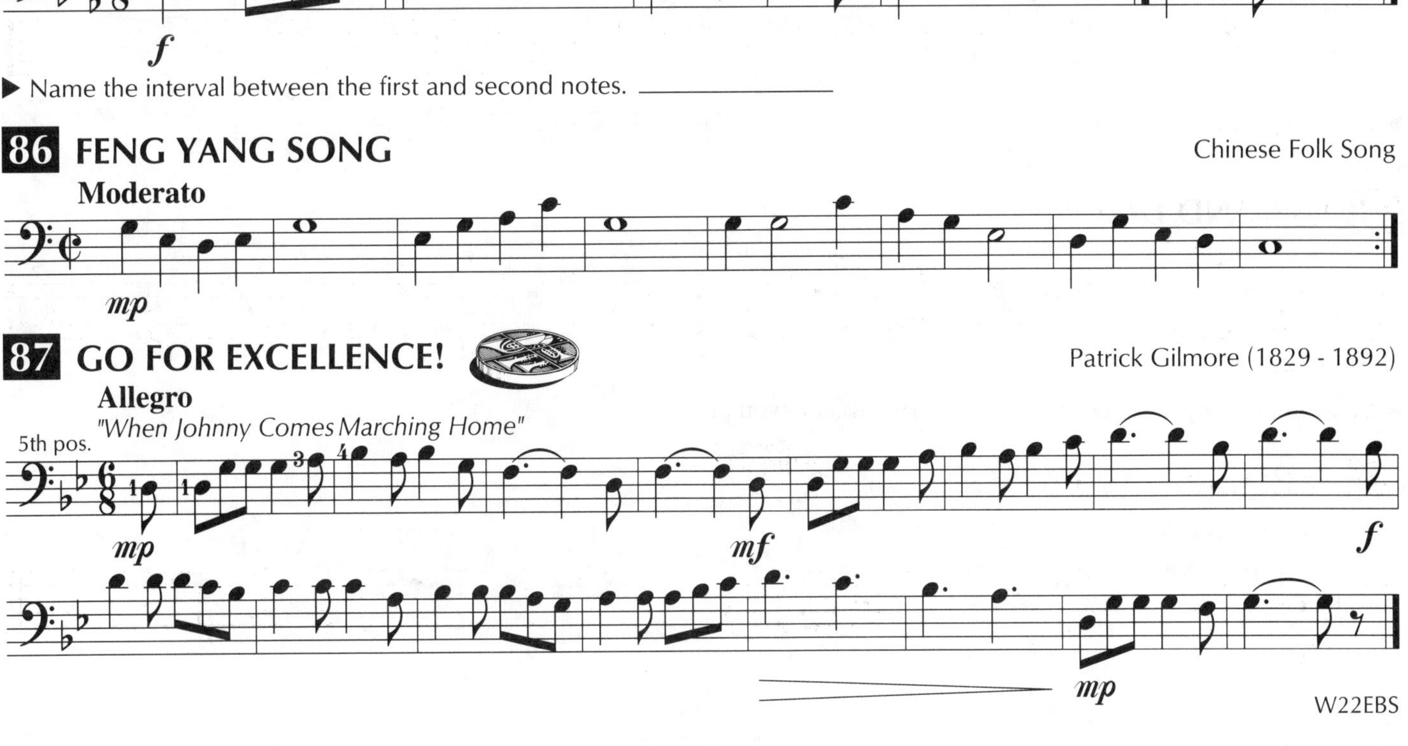

87 GO FOR EXCELLENCE!

Patrick Gilmore (1829 - 1892)

Allegro

"When Johnny Comes Marching Home"

88 LOOBY LOO
Page 41
Anonymous
Allegro
Fine
mf
D.C. al Fine
▶ Name the key in "Looby Loo."
89 THE THUNDERER
Allegretto
John Philip Sousa (1854 - 1932)
f
90 LISTEN TO THE MOCKINGBIRD
Moderato
Alice Hawthorne (1827 - 1902)
f
mp
f
91 GIVE MY REGARDS TO BROADWAY
Allegro
George M. Cohan (1878 - 1942)
to Coda
f
D.C. al Coda
Coda
92 FOR ELECTRIC BASSES ONLY
Moderato
mf
f

EIGHTH/SIXTEENTH NOTE COMBINATIONS

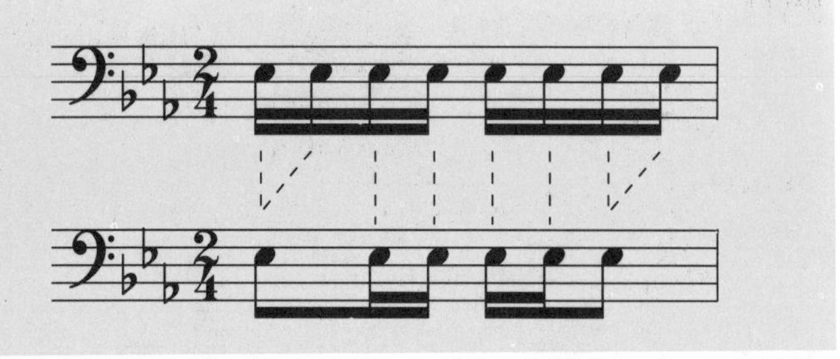

93 CHESTER - Band Arrangement

William Billings (1746 - 1800)
arr. Bruce Pearson (b. 1942)

Andante

94 STEADY AS YOU GO - Duet

Moderato

A.

mf

B.

mf

i i m i i m i i m i i m i i m i i m i i m i i
i m i m i m i m i m i m i m i m i m i m

▶ Practice both sets of right hand fingerings.

95 TIRRA LIRRA LOO

Canadian Folk Song

Moderato

▶ Write in the counting and clap the rhythm before you play.

96 GO FOR EXCELLENCE!

American Folk Song

Moderato

"Big Rock Candy Mountain"

TURKISH MARCH
from "The Ruins of Athens"

Solo with Piano Accompaniment

Ludwig van Beethoven (1770 - 1827)
arr. Bruce Pearson (b. 1942)

*Extend your left hand 1st finger to 4th fret, 2nd string to play F♯.

▶ *Extend your left hand 1st finger to 4th fret, 1st string to play B♮.

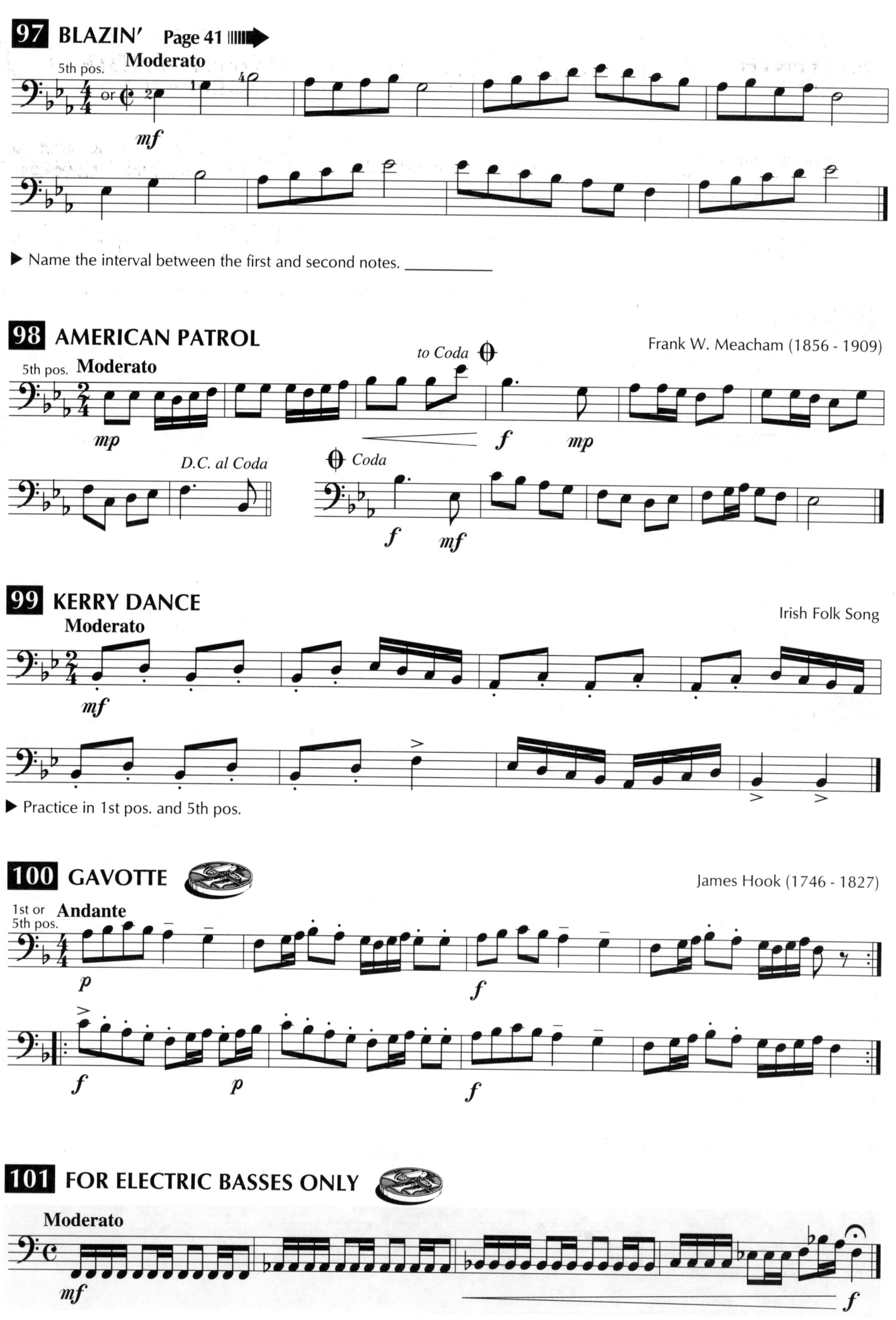
97 BLAZIN' Page 41
5th pos. Moderato
or
mf
▶ Name the interval between the first and second notes. __________
98 AMERICAN PATROL
Frank W. Meacham (1856 - 1909)
5th pos. Moderato
to Coda
mp
f
mp
D.C. al Coda
Coda
f
mf
99 KERRY DANCE
Irish Folk Song
Moderato
mf
▶ Practice in 1st pos. and 5th pos.
100 GAVOTTE
James Hook (1746 - 1827)
1st or 5th pos. Andante
p
f
f
p
f
101 FOR ELECTRIC BASSES ONLY
Moderato
mf
f

SINGLE SIXTEENTH NOTE

A single sixteenth note is half as long as an eighth note.

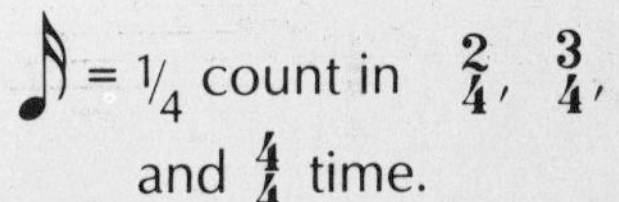

and 4/4 time.

DOTTED EIGHTH NOTE

A dot after a note adds half the value of the note.

DOTTED EIGHTH/ SIXTEENTH NOTE COMBINATION

102 DOTS OF FUN

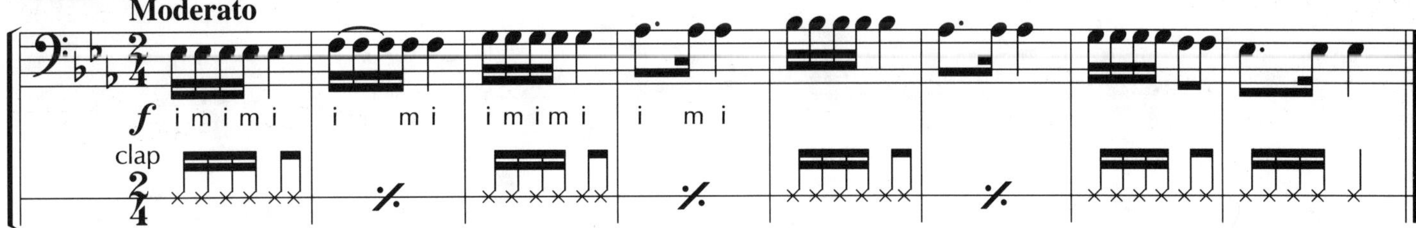

103 LITTLE BROWN JUG - Duet

Joseph Eastburn Winner (1837 - 1918)

▶ Write in the counting and clap the rhythm before you play.

104 OUR BOYS WILL SHINE TONIGHT

College Song

▶ Draw in a breath mark (') at the end of each phrase.

105 ______________________

Composer ______________________
your name

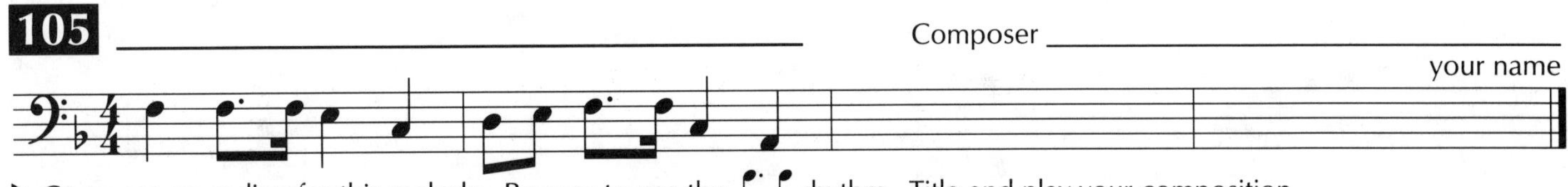

▶ Compose an ending for this melody. Be sure to use the ♪. ♬ rhythm. Title and play your composition.

106 GO FOR EXCELLENCE!

Page 41

Georges Bizet (1838 - 1875)

ENHARMONICS

F♯ = G♭
G♯ = A♭
C♯ = D♭

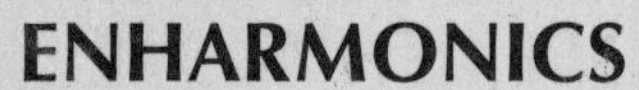

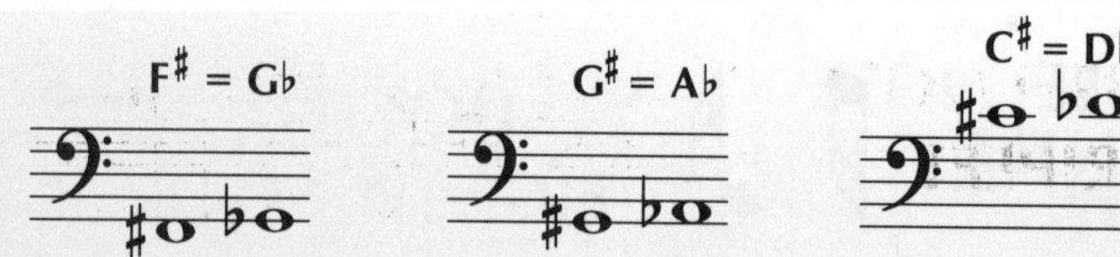

107 CUCKOO SONG

Austrian Folk Song

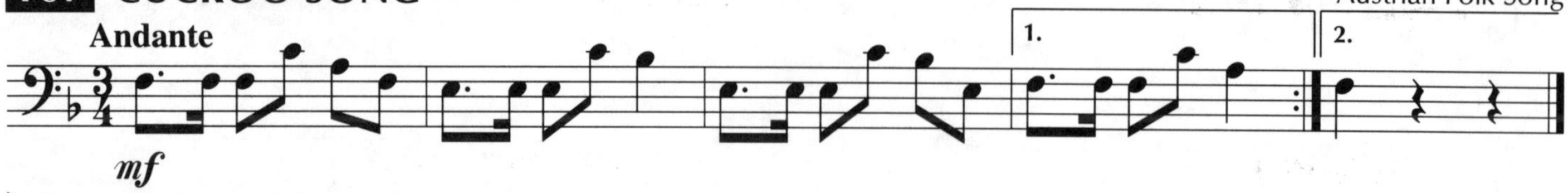

Andante
mf
1.
2.

▶ Practice in 1st and 5th pos.

108 MARCH MILITAIRE

Franz Schubert (1797 - 1828)

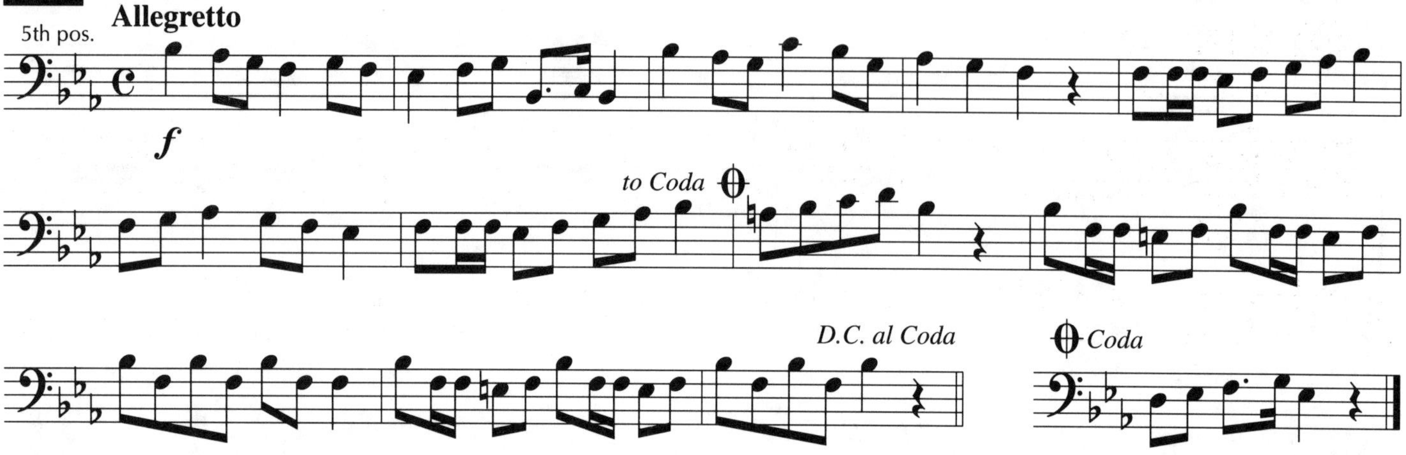

Allegretto
5th pos.
f
to Coda
D.C. al Coda
Coda

109 ST. ANTHONY CHORALE

Franz Joseph Haydn (1732 - 1809)

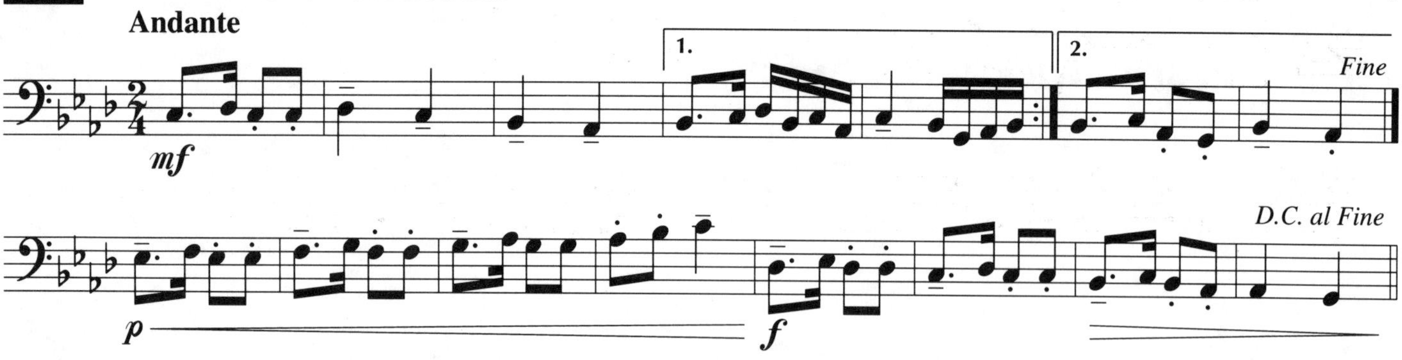

Andante
mf
1.
2.
Fine
D.C. al Fine
p
f

110 ______________________

Composer ______________________
your name

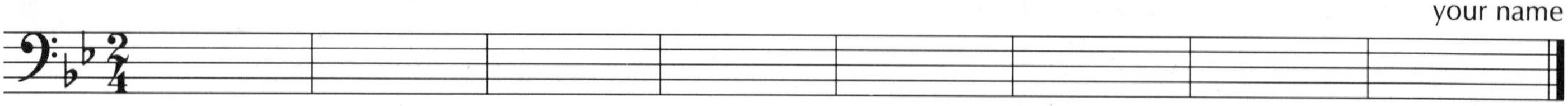

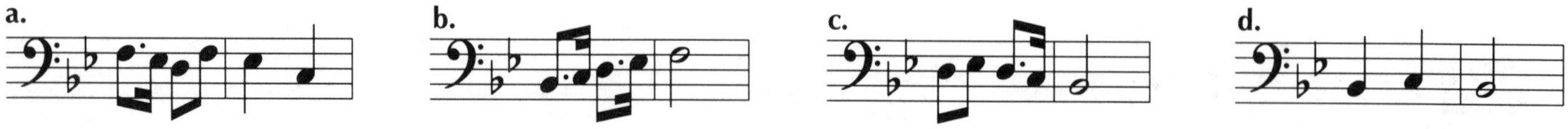

a.
b.
c.
d.

▶ Arrange these melodic pieces in any order to build a tune you like. You may use pieces more than once. Title and play your composition.

111 FOR ELECTRIC BASSES ONLY

A
F♯
G♯

B
5th pos.
1
2
3
4
D♭

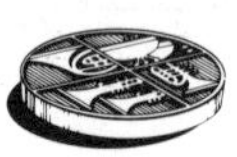

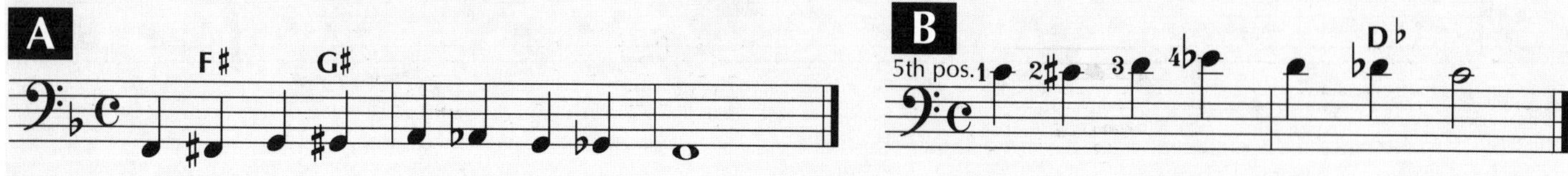

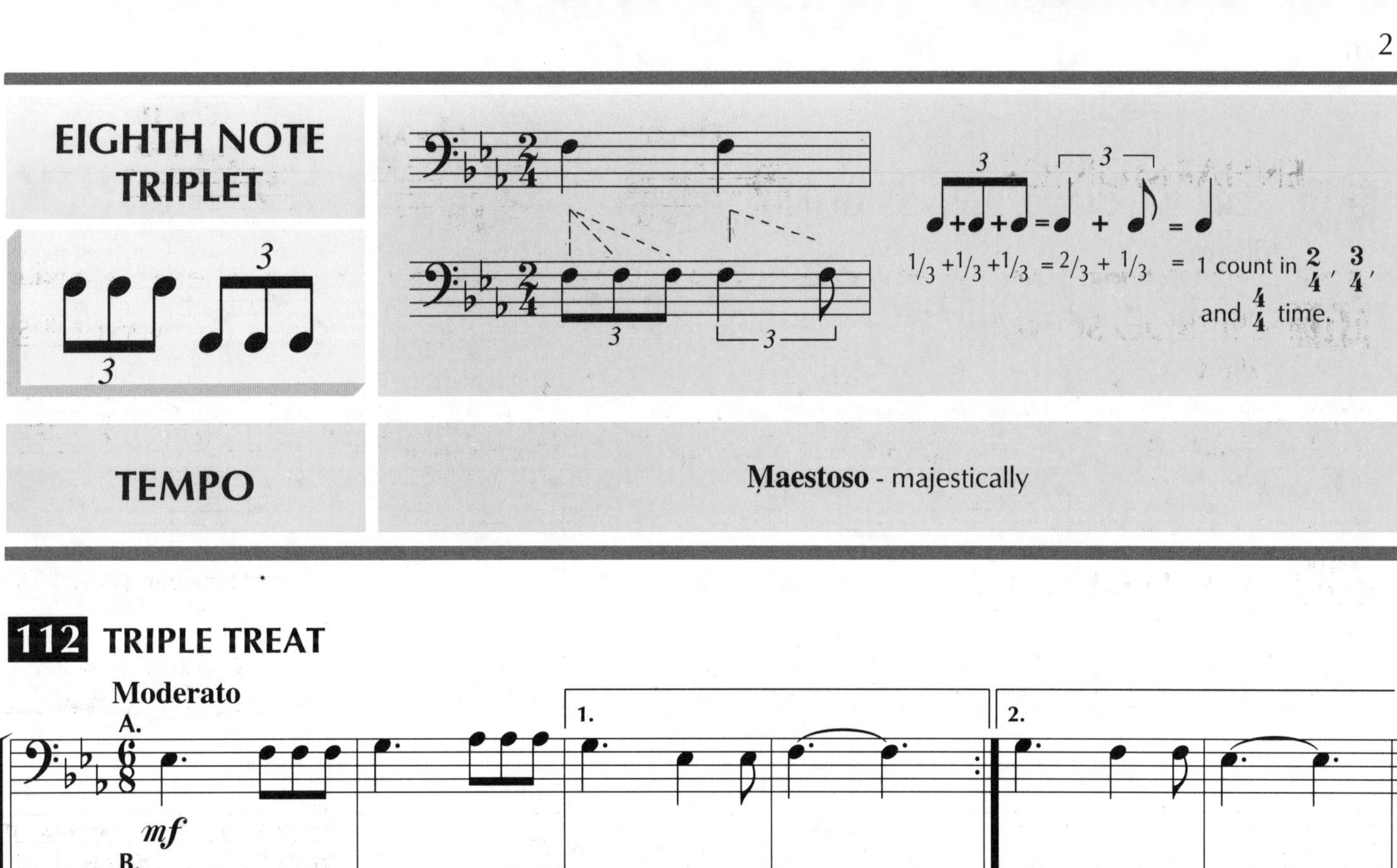
EIGHTH NOTE TRIPLET
3
3
3
3
1/3 + 1/3 + 1/3 = 2/3 + 1/3 = 1 count in 2/4, 3/4, and 4/4 time.
TEMPO
Maestoso - majestically
112 TRIPLE TREAT
Moderato
A.
B.
mf
1.
2.

113 STARS OF THE HEAVENS - Duet
Mexican Folk Song
Allegro
f

114 LIGHT CAVALRY OVERTURE
Franz von Suppé (1819 - 1895)
Maestoso
f
115 GO FOR EXCELLENCE!
Charles Gounod (1818 - 1893)
Maestoso
"Soldiers' Chorus from Faust"
mf

116 HERE WE COME A-WASSAILING

English Folk Song

Allegro

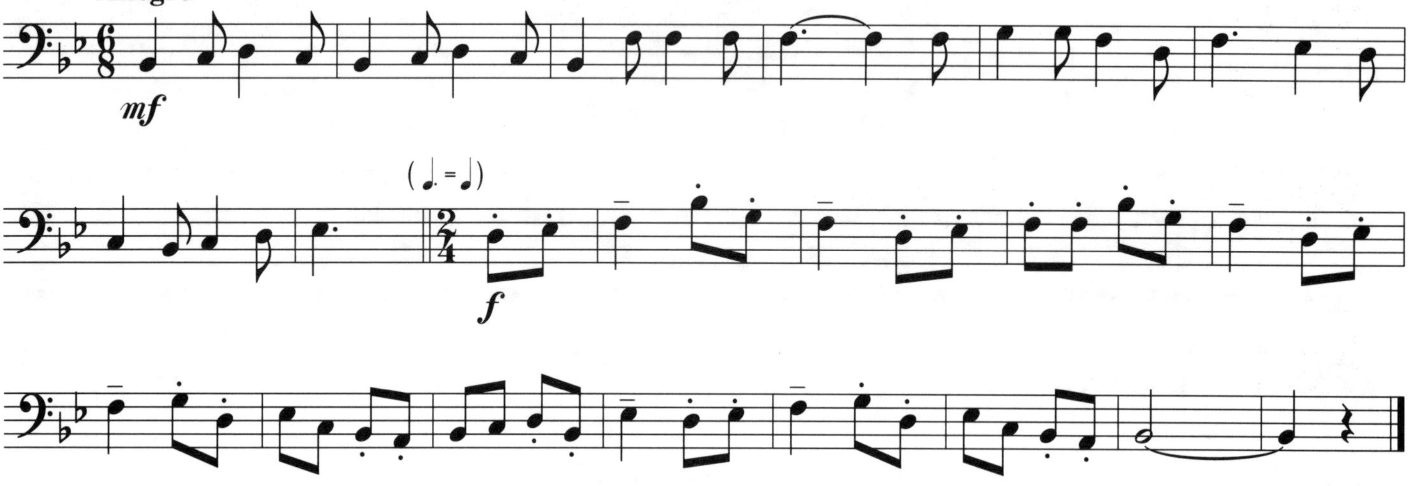
mf
(♩. = ♩)
f

117 THEME FROM "ZAMPA"

Ferdinand Herold (1791 - 1833)

Allegro

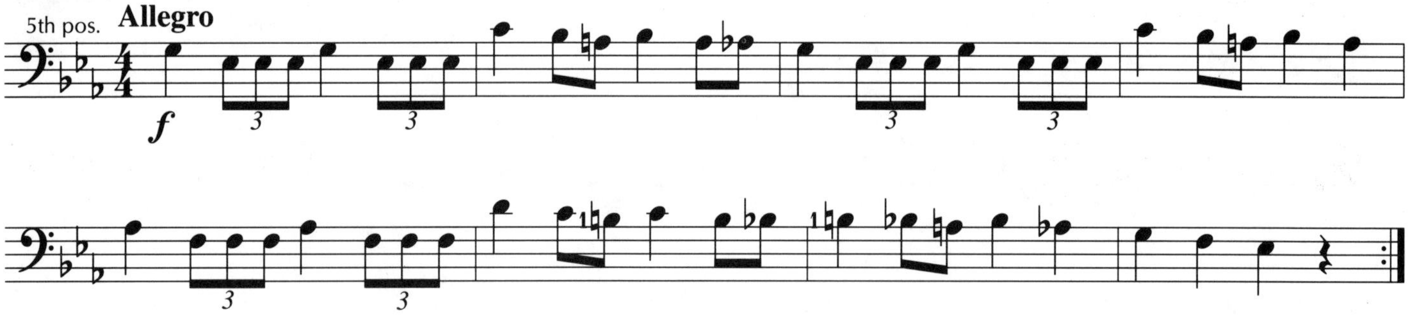
5th pos.
f
3

118 GO FOR EXCELLENCE!

Peter Ilyich Tchaikovsky (1840 - 1893)

Allegretto

"March from the Nutcracker"

5th pos.
mf
3
1.
2.

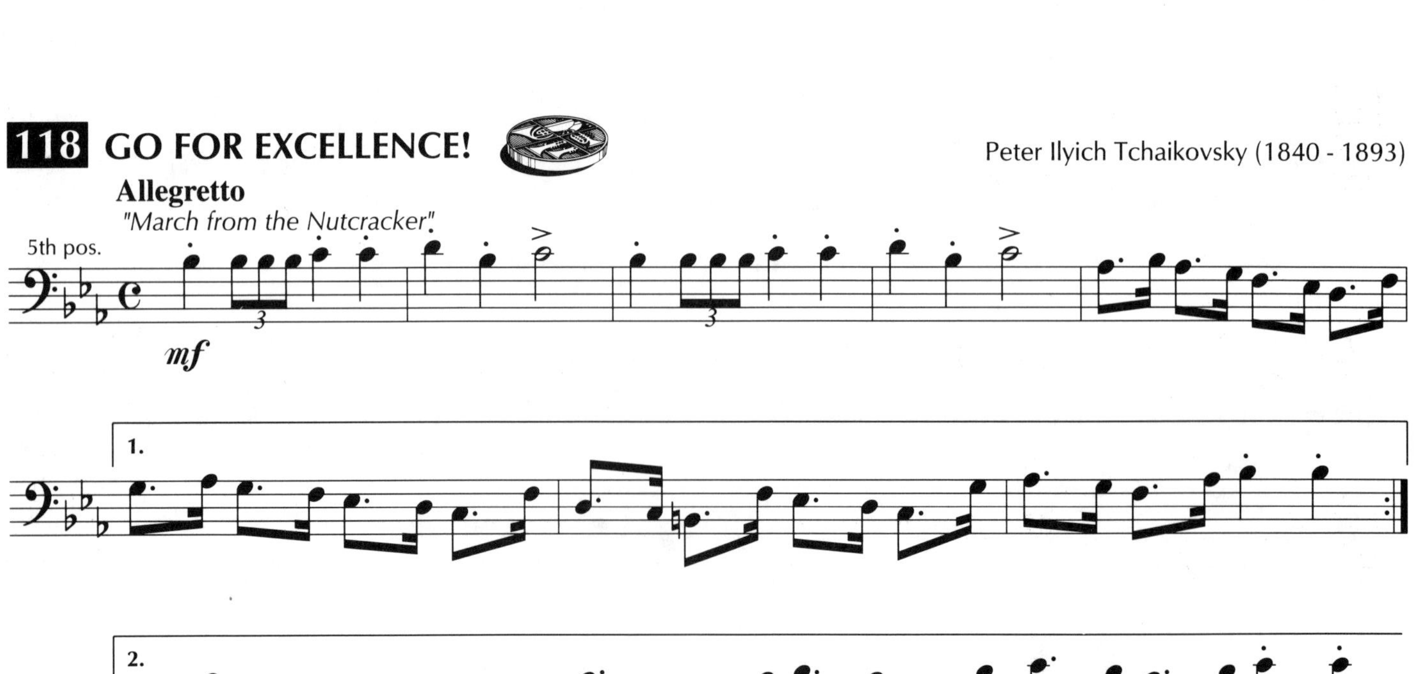

CABO RICO

Band Arrangement

Chuck Elledge (b. 1961)

RUDIMENTAL REGIMENT

Band Arrangement

Bruce Pearson (b. 1942)
and Chuck Elledge (b. 1961)

46
47
48
49
50
51
52
53 - 56
4
57
58
59
mf
f
60
61
62
63
64
65
mf
66
67
68
69
70
mp
f
71
72
73
74
75
mf
76
77
78
79
80
mp
f
81
82
83
84
85
86
87
88
89
90
91

SUMMER'S RAIN

Band Arrangement

Chuck Elledge (b. 1961)

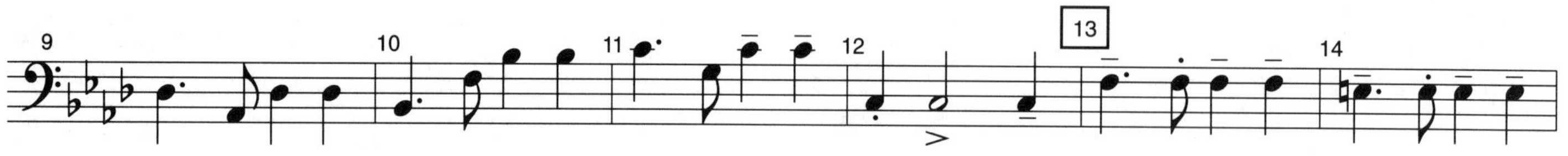

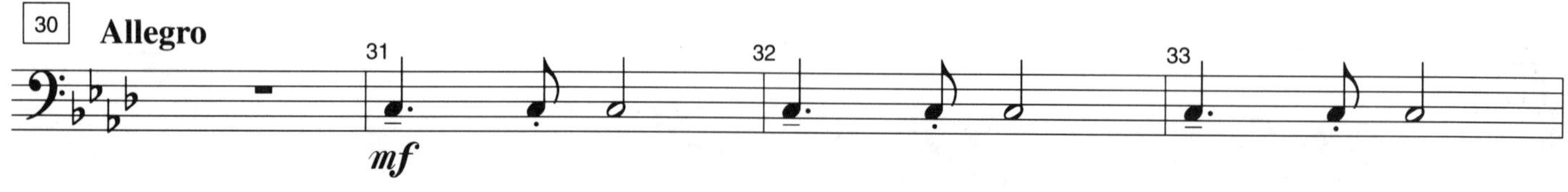

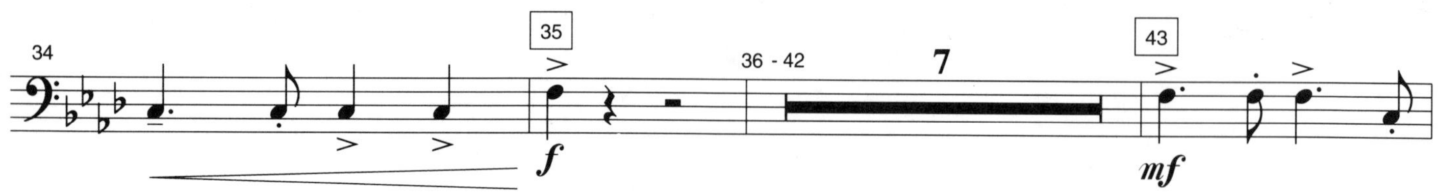

51
59
f
67
Andante
3
p
72
p
mp
f
p
rit.

FRENCH MARKET BUZZARDS MARCH

Band Arrangement

Liberato Gallo
arr. Wendy Barden (b. 1955)

47 48 *f* 49 1. 50 2.

51 52 53 54 55 - 57 3

58 1st pos. *f* 59 60 61 62

63 64 65 66 *Fine* 67 *p*

68 69 70 71 72

73 74 *mf* 75 76 77 78

79 *f* 80 81 82

83 - 90 8 91 - 97 7 98 *mf* 99 100 101

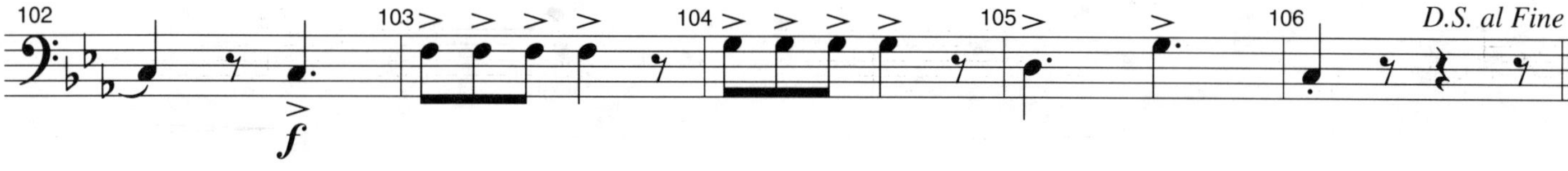

ROMANZA

Ensemble

Electric Bass

Ludwig van Beethoven, Op. 40 (1770 - 1827)
arr. Janice Strobl Kersey (b. 1959)

HORNPIPE from "Water Music"

Ensemble

Electric Bass

George Frideric Handel (1685 - 1759)
arr. Janice Strobl Kersey (b. 1959)

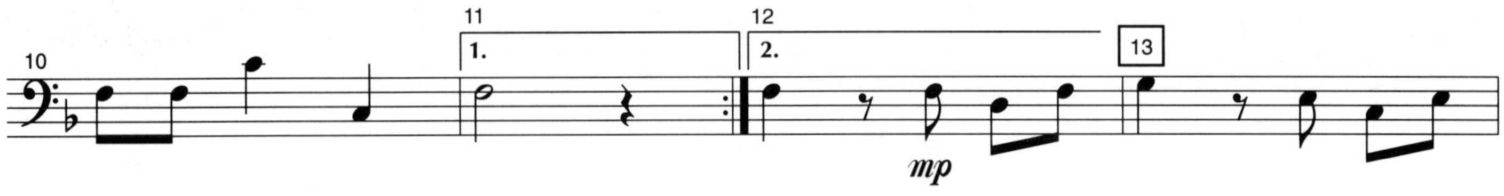

MOVIN' ON

Solo with Piano Accompaniment

Kevin Daley (b. 1957)

17
5th pos.
18
19
20
21
22
23
24
25
26
27
28
29
30
31
32
D.C. al Coda
(1st pos.)
Coda
33

EXCELLERATORS- FOR ELECTRIC BASSES ONLY

EXCELLERATORS - For Electric Basses Only

SCALE STUDIES

B♭ MAJOR SCALE

G HARMONIC MINOR SCALE

E♭ MAJOR SCALE

C HARMONIC MINOR SCALE

▶ * Extend your left hand 1st finger to 4th fret, 1st string to play upper octave B♮'s.

SCALE STUDIES

RHYTHM STUDIES

Rhythm Studies

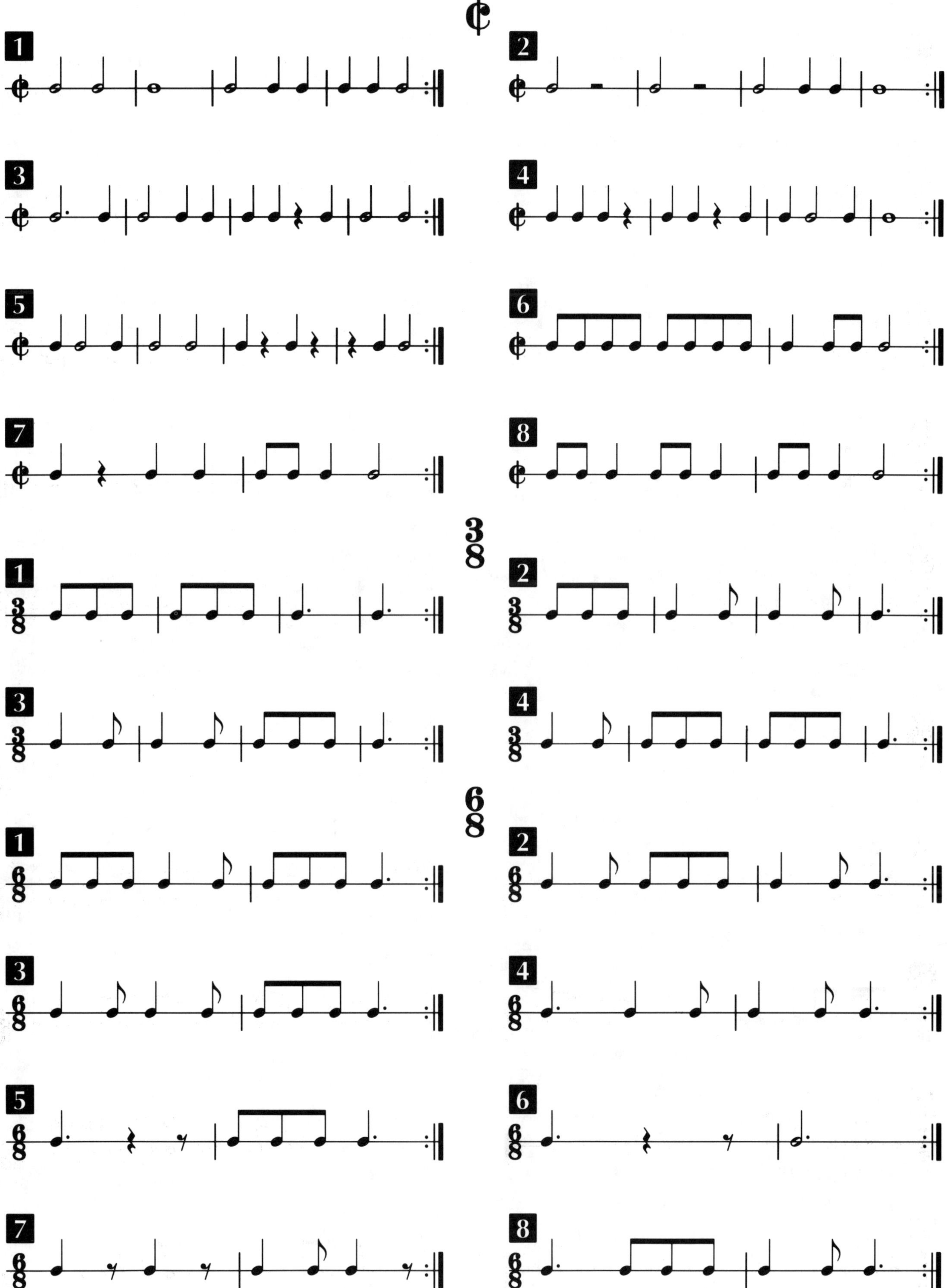

Glossary/Index

Accelerando (*accel.*) (p. 6) .... gradually increase the tempo

Alla Breve (p.13) .... same as cut time

Allegretto (p.10) .... light and lively; slightly slower than **Allegro**

Barden, Wendy (pp. 34-35) ..... American music educator and arranger *(b. 1955)*

Beethoven, Ludwig van (p. 36)....... German composer *(1770-1827)*

Billings, William (p. 21) .... American composer *(1746-1800)*

Bizet, Georges (pp.12, 25) .... French composer *(1838-1875)*

Brahms, Johannes (p. 8) .... German composer *(1833-1897)*

Breath Mark (p.18) ’ .... small mark used to show the end of a phrase

Chord (pp. 2-4, 9, 14, 18) .... two or more pitches sounded at the same time

Chromatic Scale (pp.15, 43) .... scale of half steps

Cohan, George M. (p. 20) .... American composer *(1878-1942)*

Countermelody (p. 12) .... a less important melody that can be played along with the main melody

Crüger, Johann (p. 3) .... German composer *(1598-1662)*

Cut Time (***alla breve***) (p.13) ¢ or 2/2 .. a time signature indicating two counts in each measure, the half note gets one count

Da Capo al Coda (p.16) ***D. C. al Coda*** . go back to the beginning and play until the coda sign (⊕). When you reach the coda sign, skip to the ***Coda*** (⊕)

Dal Segno al Fine (p. 7) ***D. S. al Fine*** .. go back to the 𝄋 sign and play until the ***Fine***

Daley, Kevin (pp. 38-39) .... American composer and music educator *(b. 1957)*

Dampening (p. 2) .... technique used to stop the vibrations of a string after it is plucked

Elledge, Chuck (pp. 7, 16, 29-33) ..... American composer/arranger *(b. 1961)*

Enharmonics (pp.10, 14-15, 26) .... notes that sound the same but are written differently

Fifth Position (p.10) .... left hand is positioned so that first finger plays fifth fret notes, second finger plays sixth fret notes, third finger plays seventh fret notes, and fourth finger plays eighth fret notes

First Position (p. 2) .... left hand is positioned so that first finger plays first fret notes, second finger plays second fret notes, third finger plays third fret notes, and fourth finger plays fourth fret notes

Foster, Stephen (p. 9) .... American composer *(1826-1864)*

Gallo, Liberato (pp. 34-35) .... Italian composer

Gilmore, Patrick (p.19) .... American composer *(1829-1892)*

Glière, Reinhold (p.14) .... Russian composer *(1875-1956)*

Gounod, Charles (p. 27) .... French composer *(1818-1893)*

Handel, George Frideric (p. 37) ...... German composer *(1685-1759)*

Hawthorne, Alice (p. 20)............. American composer *(1827-1902)*

Haydn, Franz Joseph (pp. 10, 26) ...... Austrian composer *(1732-1809)*

Herold, Ferdinand (p. 28) .... French composer *(1791-1833)*

Hook, James (p. 24) .... English composer *(1746-1827)*

Hopkins, John H., Jr. (p.17) .... American composer *(1820-1891)*

i (Index Finger) .... one of two right hand fingers used to pluck the strings on a bass

Interval (p. 5) .... distance between two notes

Jessel, Léon (p.10) .... German composer *(1871-1942)*

Kersey, Janice Strobl (pp. 36-37) ...... American music editor and arranger *(b. 1959)*

Legato (p. 11) .... play as smoothly as possible

m (Middle Finger) .... one of two right hand fingers used to pluck the strings on a bass

Maestoso (p. 27) .... majestically

Meacham, Frank W. (p. 24) .... American composer *(1856-1909)*

Melody (p.12) .... an organized succession of tones

Monophony (p. 9) .... a single unaccompanied melody

Mozart, Wolfgang Amadeus (pp. 3,11) . Austrian composer *(1756-1791)*

Open String .... string plucked by right hand without being pressed down by left hand

Pearson, Bruce .... American music educator/composer/arranger *(b. 1942)*

Polyphony (p. 9) .... two or more melodies played at the same time

Schubert, Franz (p. 26) .... Austrian composer *(1797-1828)*

Sibelius, Jean (p. 17) .... Finnish composer *(1865-1957)*

Sousa, John Philip (pp. 13, 15, 20) .... American composer *(1854-1932)*

Staccato (p. 10) ♩̣ .... a dot placed above or below note meaning to play short and detached

Suppé, Franz von (p. 27) .... Belgian composer *(1819-1895)*

Syncopation (p. 5) ♪ ♩ ♪ (>) .... a rhythmic effect which places emphasis on a weak or unaccented part of the measure

Tacet .... do not play

Tchaikovsky, Peter Ilyich (pp. 11, 28) .. Russian composer *(1840-1893)*

Tenuto (p. 11) ♩̱ .... a line placed above or below note meaning to sustain for full value

Texture (p.12) .... the character of a composition as determined by the relationship of its melodies, countermelodies, and/or chords

Winner, Joseph Eastburn (p. 25) ...... American composer *(1837-1918)*

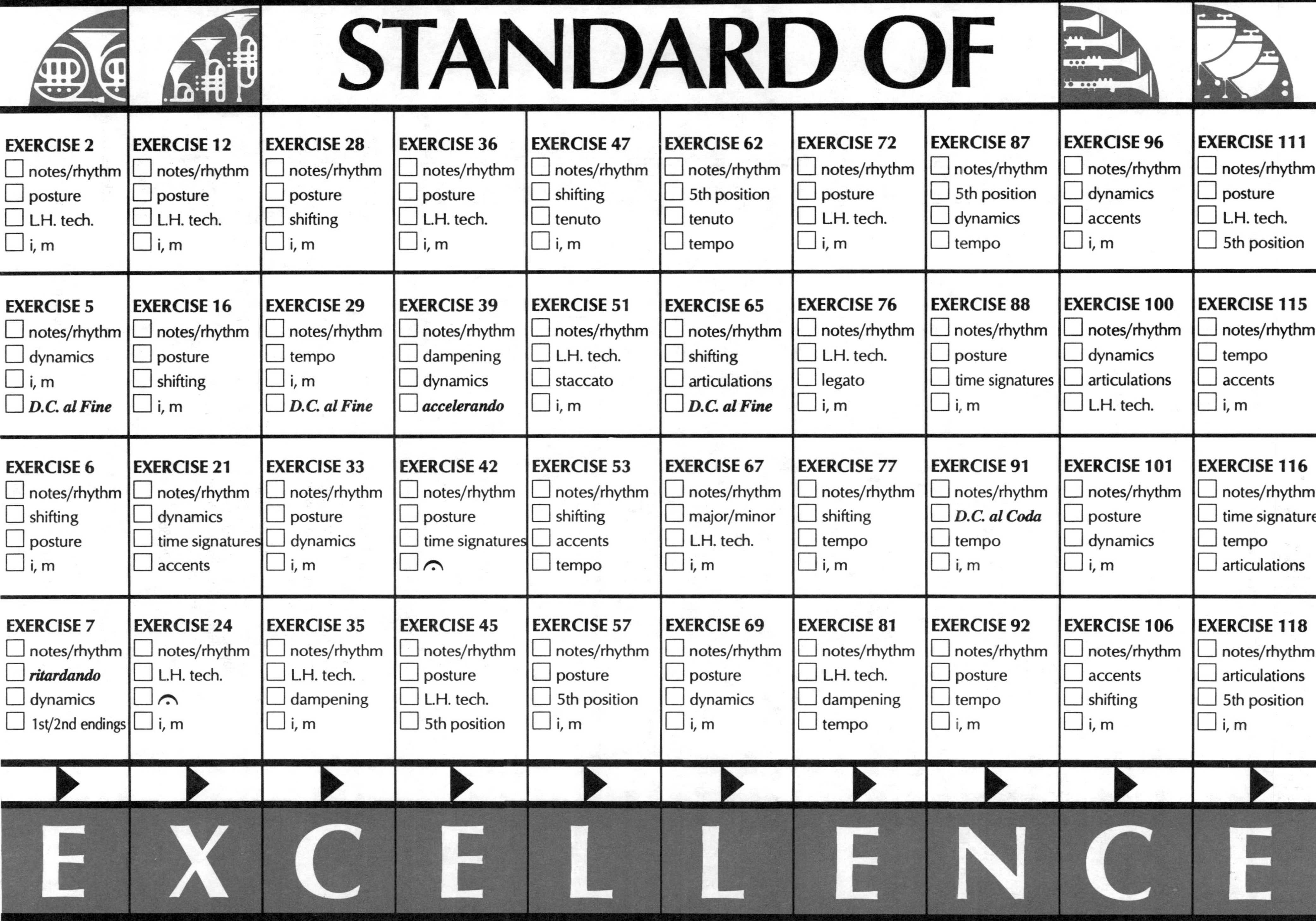

STANDARD OF EXCELLENCE

EXERCISE 2 ☐ notes/rhythm ☐ posture ☐ L.H. tech. ☐ i, m	**EXERCISE 12** ☐ notes/rhythm ☐ posture ☐ L.H. tech. ☐ i, m	**EXERCISE 28** ☐ notes/rhythm ☐ posture ☐ shifting ☐ i, m	**EXERCISE 36** ☐ notes/rhythm ☐ posture ☐ L.H. tech. ☐ i, m	**EXERCISE 47** ☐ notes/rhythm ☐ shifting ☐ tenuto ☐ i, m	**EXERCISE 62** ☐ notes/rhythm ☐ 5th position ☐ tenuto ☐ tempo	**EXERCISE 72** ☐ notes/rhythm ☐ posture ☐ L.H. tech. ☐ i, m	**EXERCISE 87** ☐ notes/rhythm ☐ 5th position ☐ dynamics ☐ tempo	**EXERCISE 96** ☐ notes/rhythm ☐ dynamics ☐ accents ☐ i, m	**EXERCISE 111** ☐ notes/rhythm ☐ posture ☐ L.H. tech. ☐ 5th position
EXERCISE 5 ☐ notes/rhythm ☐ dynamics ☐ i, m ☐ ***D.C. al Fine***	**EXERCISE 16** ☐ notes/rhythm ☐ posture ☐ shifting ☐ i, m	**EXERCISE 29** ☐ notes/rhythm ☐ tempo ☐ i, m ☐ ***D.C. al Fine***	**EXERCISE 39** ☐ notes/rhythm ☐ dampening ☐ dynamics ☐ ***accelerando***	**EXERCISE 51** ☐ notes/rhythm ☐ L.H. tech. ☐ staccato ☐ i, m	**EXERCISE 65** ☐ notes/rhythm ☐ shifting ☐ articulations ☐ ***D.C. al Fine***	**EXERCISE 76** ☐ notes/rhythm ☐ L.H. tech. ☐ legato ☐ i, m	**EXERCISE 88** ☐ notes/rhythm ☐ posture ☐ time signatures ☐ i, m	**EXERCISE 100** ☐ notes/rhythm ☐ dynamics ☐ articulations ☐ L.H. tech.	**EXERCISE 115** ☐ notes/rhythm ☐ tempo ☐ accents ☐ i, m
EXERCISE 6 ☐ notes/rhythm ☐ shifting ☐ posture ☐ i, m	**EXERCISE 21** ☐ notes/rhythm ☐ dynamics ☐ time signatures ☐ accents	**EXERCISE 33** ☐ notes/rhythm ☐ posture ☐ dynamics ☐ i, m	**EXERCISE 42** ☐ notes/rhythm ☐ posture ☐ time signatures ☐ 𝄐	**EXERCISE 53** ☐ notes/rhythm ☐ shifting ☐ accents ☐ tempo	**EXERCISE 67** ☐ notes/rhythm ☐ major/minor ☐ L.H. tech. ☐ i, m	**EXERCISE 77** ☐ notes/rhythm ☐ shifting ☐ tempo ☐ i, m	**EXERCISE 91** ☐ notes/rhythm ☐ ***D.C. al Coda*** ☐ tempo ☐ i, m	**EXERCISE 101** ☐ notes/rhythm ☐ posture ☐ dynamics ☐ i, m	**EXERCISE 116** ☐ notes/rhythm ☐ time signatures ☐ tempo ☐ articulations
EXERCISE 7 ☐ notes/rhythm ☐ ***ritardando*** ☐ dynamics ☐ 1st/2nd endings	**EXERCISE 24** ☐ notes/rhythm ☐ L.H. tech. ☐ 𝄐 ☐ i, m	**EXERCISE 35** ☐ notes/rhythm ☐ L.H. tech. ☐ dampening ☐ i, m	**EXERCISE 45** ☐ notes/rhythm ☐ posture ☐ L.H. tech. ☐ 5th position	**EXERCISE 57** ☐ notes/rhythm ☐ posture ☐ 5th position ☐ i, m	**EXERCISE 69** ☐ notes/rhythm ☐ posture ☐ dynamics ☐ i, m	**EXERCISE 81** ☐ notes/rhythm ☐ L.H. tech. ☐ dampening ☐ tempo	**EXERCISE 92** ☐ notes/rhythm ☐ posture ☐ tempo ☐ i, m	**EXERCISE 106** ☐ notes/rhythm ☐ accents ☐ shifting ☐ i, m	**EXERCISE 118** ☐ notes/rhythm ☐ articulations ☐ 5th position ☐ i, m

The Electric Bass

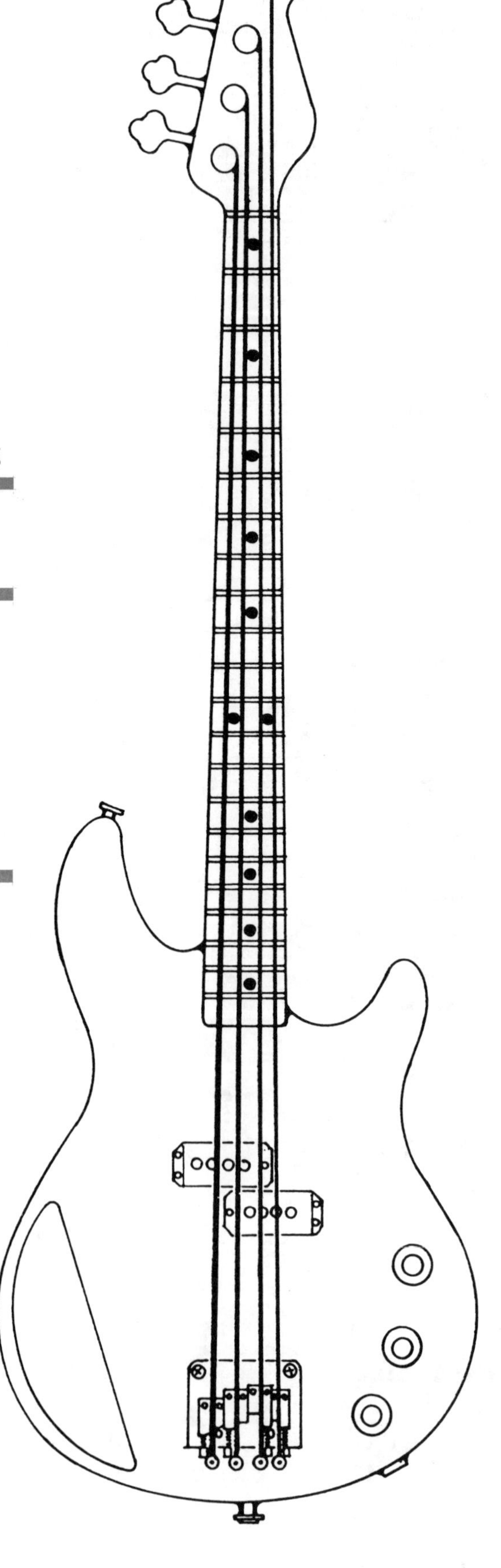

Electric bass Checklist

- ☐ Standing or sitting straight
- ☐ Shoulders relaxed
- ☐ Instrument properly positioned
- ☐ Right forearm and hand positioned properly
- ☐ Right hand fingers curved
- ☐ Left thumb positioned correctly behind neck
- ☐ Left wrist and fingers positioned and arched properly
- ☐ Right hand placed between bridge and end of fingerboard
- ☐ Plucking action correct
- ☐ Finger resting against next string after sounding string
- ☐ Index and middle finger producing same sound when plucking string

Electric Bass Survival Kit

- ☐ extra set of strings
- ☐ soft, lint-free cloth
- ☐ tuning device (electronic tuner, tuning fork, or pitch pipe)
- ☐ fingernail clipper
- ☐ extra audio cable
- ☐ pencil
- ☐ method book
- ☐ band music
- ☐ music stand